When I can see what is in the SHADOW I will...

Heal My Inner Child
Experience Personal Growth
Become My Authentic Self

This Shadow Work Journal Belongs to:

Make it Happen Publishing Inc.

www.mihpublishing.com
Send all inquires to books@mihpublishing.com

Daily Illumination Prompt:

Today, I am deeply grateful that this person has helped me to bring light to my shadow.

(enter the same person from your daily shadow work)

Daily Shadow Work Prompt:

Who evoked the biggest emotional response from you today? Who triggered you?

(family member/friend/stranger/movie character etc.)

SHADOW INTEGRATION:

Below, accept & reclaim the shadow chacterter traits that had the greatest emotional impact on you from your daily shadow work AND include what the purpose or role those traits play in your life now.
(defense mechanism/self preservation etc.)

Beacuse of you, I now realize that I AM:

Describe 5 of the person's character traits:

-
-
-
-
-

Now go back and add the words "I AM" in front of each character trait above.

Which trait evoked the greatest resistance in you? Which did you feel defensive about? Allow the feelings to flow through you with self awareness of how you're feeling.

What is the oldest memory you have of when you felt that same way?
(the underlying trauma that the feelings stem from)

What would you say to your inner child if you could be there during the underlying trauma with the wisdom you have now. Show love & nurture your inner child.

STEP 3 — Cut along the dotted line, thank the person who triggered your shadow work, read out loud what you wrote in STEP 2 . Lastly release your negative resistence to your shadow by burning STEP 1

DATE _____/_____/_____   **STEP** 2 | DATE _____/_____/_____   **STEP** 1

Daily Illumination Prompt:

Today, I am deeply grateful that this person has helped me to bring light to my shadow.

┌─────────────────────────────────────┐
│   │
│   │
└─────────────────────────────────────┘

(enter the same person from your daily shadow work)

Daily Shadow Work Prompt:

Who evoked the biggest emotional response from you today? Who triggered you?

┌─────────────────────────────────────┐
│   │
│   │
└─────────────────────────────────────┘

(family member/friend/stranger/movie character etc.)

SHADOW INTEGRATION:

Below, accept & reclaim the shadow chacterter traits that had the greatest emotional impact on you from your daily shadow work AND include what the purpose or role those traits play in your life now.

(defense mechanism/self preservation etc.)

Beacuse of you, I now realize that I AM:

Describe 5 of the person's character traits:

-
-
-
-
-

Now go back and add the words "I AM" in front of each character trait above.

Which trait evoked the greatest resistance in you? Which did you feel defensive about? Allow the feelings to flow through you with self awareness of how you're feeling.

What is the oldest memory you have of when you felt that same way?
(the underlying trauma that the feelings stem from)

What would you say to your inner child if you could be there during the underyling trauma with the wisdom you have now. Show love & nurture your inner child.

STEP 3 — Cut along the dotted line, thank the person who triggered your shadow work, read out loud what you wrote in STEP 2 . Lastly release your negative resistence to your shadow by burning STEP 1

DATE ____/____/____   **STEP 2** | DATE ____/____/____   **STEP 1**

Daily Illumination Prompt:

Today, I am deeply grateful that this person has helped me to bring light to my shadow.

[ ]

(enter the same person from your daily shadow work)

Daily Shadow Work Prompt:

Who evoked the biggest emotional response from you today? Who triggered you?

[ ]

(family member/friend/stranger/movie character etc.)

SHADOW INTEGRATION:

Below, accept & reclaim the shadow chacterter traits that had the greatest emotional impact on you from your daily shadow work AND include what the purpose or role those traits play in your life now.

(defense mechanism/self preservation etc.)

Beacuse of you, I now realize that I AM:

Describe 5 of the person's character traits:

- -
- -
- -
- -
- -

Now go back and add the words "I AM" in front of each character trait above.

Which trait evoked the greatest resistance in you? Which did you feel defensive about? Allow the feelings to flow through you with self awareness of how you're feeling.

What is the oldest memory you have of when you felt that same way?
(the underlying trauma that the feelings stem from)

What would you say to your inner child if you could be there during the underyling trauma with the wisdom you have now. Show love & nurture your inner child.

STEP 3 — Cut along the dotted line, thank the person who triggered your shadow work, read out loud what you wrote in STEP 2 . Lastly release your negative resistence to your shadow by burning STEP 1

DATE ____/____/____   STEP **2**   DATE ____/____/____   STEP **1**

Daily Illumination Prompt:

Today, I am deeply grateful that this person has helped me to bring light to my shadow.

[ ]

(enter the same person from your daily shadow work)

Daily Shadow Work Prompt:

Who evoked the biggest emotional response from you today? Who triggered you?

[ ]

(family member/friend/stranger/movie character etc.)

SHADOW INTEGRATION:

Below, accept & reclaim the shadow chacterter traits that had the greatest emotional impact on you from your daily shadow work AND include what the purpose or role those traits play in your life now.

(defense mechanism/self preservation etc.)

Beacuse of you, I now realize that I AM:

Describe 5 of the person's character traits:

- -
- -
- -
- -
- -

Now go back and add the words "I AM" in front of each character trait above.

Which trait evoked the greatest resistance in you? Which did you feel defensive about? Allow the feelings to flow through you with self awareness of how you're feeling.

What is the oldest memory you have of when you felt that same way?
(the underlying trauma that the feelings stem from)

What would you say to your inner child if you could be there during the underyling trauma with the wisdom you have now. Show love & nurture your inner child.

STEP **3** – Cut along the dotted line, thank the person who triggered your shadow work, read out loud what you wrote in STEP 2 . Lastly release your negative resistence to your shadow by burning STEP 1

Daily Illumination Prompt:

Today, I am deeply grateful that this person has helped me to bring light to my shadow.

[ ]

(enter the same person from your daily shadow work)

SHADOW INTEGRATION:

Below, accept & reclaim the shadow chacterter traits that had the greatest emotional impact on you from your daily shadow work AND include what the purpose or role those traits play in your life now.

(defense mechanism/self preservation etc.)

Beacuse of you, I now realize that I AM:

Daily Shadow Work Prompt:

Who evoked the biggest emotional response from you today? Who triggered you?

[ ]

(family member/friend/stranger/movie character etc.)

Describe 5 of the person's character traits:

-
-
-
-
-

Now go back and add the words "I AM" in front of each character trait above.

Which trait evoked the greatest resistance in you? Which did you feel defensive about? Allow the feelings to flow through you with self awareness of how you're feeling.

What is the oldest memory you have of when you felt that same way?
(the underlying trauma that the feelings stem from)

What would you say to your inner child if you could be there during the underlying trauma with the wisdom you have now. Show love & nurture your inner child.

STEP 3 — Cut along the dotted line, thank the person who triggered your shadow work, read out loud what you wrote in STEP 2 . Lastly release your negative resistence to your shadow by burning STEP 1

DATE ____/____/____   **STEP 2**   DATE ____/____/____   **STEP 1**

Daily Illumination Prompt:

Today, I am deeply grateful that this person has helped me to bring light to my shadow.

(enter the same person from your daily shadow work)

Daily Shadow Work Prompt:

Who evoked the biggest emotional response from you today? Who triggered you?

(family member/friend/stranger/movie character etc.)

SHADOW INTEGRATION:

Below, accept & reclaim the shadow chacterter traits that had the greatest emotional impact on you from your daily shadow work AND include what the purpose or role those traits play in your life now.

(defense mechanism/self preservation etc.)

Beacuse of you, I now realize that I AM:

Describe 5 of the person's character traits:

-
-
-
-
-

Now go back and add the words "I AM" in front of each character trait above.

Which trait evoked the greatest resistance in you? Which did you feel defensive about? Allow the feelings to flow through you with self awareness of how you're feeling.

What is the oldest memory you have of when you felt that same way?
(the underlying trauma that the feelings stem from)

What would you say to your inner child if you could be there during the underlying trauma with the wisdom you have now. Show love & nurture your inner child.

STEP **3** — Cut along the dotted line, thank the person who triggered your shadow work, read out loud what you wrote in STEP 2 . Lastly release your negative resistence to your shadow by burning STEP 1

DATE ____/____/____   STEP 2

Daily Illumination Prompt:

Today, I am deeply grateful that this person has helped me to bring light to my shadow.

```
┌─────────────────────────────────────┐
│                                       │
│                                       │
└─────────────────────────────────────┘
```

(enter the same person from your daily shadow work)

SHADOW INTEGRATION:

Below, accept & reclaim the shadow chacterter traits that had the greatest emotional impact on you from your daily shadow work AND include what the purpose or role those traits play in your life now.

(defense mechanism/self preservation etc.)

Beacuse of you, I now realize that I AM:

DATE ____/____/____   STEP 1

Daily Shadow Work Prompt:

Who evoked the biggest emotional response from you today? Who triggered you?

```
┌─────────────────────────────────────┐
│                                       │
│                                       │
└─────────────────────────────────────┘
```

(family member/friend/stranger/movie character etc.)

Describe 5 of the person's character traits:

-
-
-
-
-

Now go back and add the words "I AM" in front of each character trait above.

Which trait evoked the greatest resistance in you? Which did you feel defensive about? Allow the feelings to flow through you with self awareness of how you're feeling.

What is the oldest memory you have of when you felt that same way?
(the underlying trauma that the feelings stem from)

What would you say to your inner child if you could be there during the underyling trauma with the wisdom you have now. Show love & nurture your inner child.

STEP 3 — Cut along the dotted line, thank the person who triggered your shadow work, read out loud what you wrote in STEP 2 . Lastly release your negative resistence to your shadow by burning STEP 1

DATE ____/____/____   **STEP 2** | DATE ____/____/____   **STEP 1**

Daily Illumination Prompt:

Today, I am deeply grateful that this person has helped me to bring light to my shadow.

```
┌─────────────────────────────────────┐
│                                       │
│                                       │
└─────────────────────────────────────┘
```

(enter the same person from your daily shadow work)

Daily Shadow Work Prompt:

Who evoked the biggest emotional response from you today? Who triggered you?

```
┌─────────────────────────────────────┐
│                                       │
│                                       │
└─────────────────────────────────────┘
```

(family member/friend/stranger/movie character etc.)

SHADOW INTEGRATION:

Below, accept & reclaim the shadow chacterter traits that had the greatest emotional impact on you from your daily shadow work AND include what the purpose or role those traits play in your life now.
(defense mechanism/self preservation etc.)

Beacuse of you, I now realize that I AM:

Describe 5 of the person's character traits:

-

-

-

-

-

Now go back and add the words "I AM" in front of each character trait above.

Which trait evoked the greatest resistance in you? Which did you feel defensive about? Allow the feelings to flow through you with self awareness of how you're feeling.

What is the oldest memory you have of when you felt that same way?
(the underlying trauma that the feelings stem from)

What would you say to your inner child if you could be there during the underyling trauma with the wisdom you have now. Show love & nurture your inner child.

STEP 3 – Cut along the dotted line, thank the person who triggered your shadow work, read out loud what you wrote in STEP 2 . Lastly release your negative resistence to your shadow by burning STEP 1

DATE ____/____/____   **STEP 2** | DATE ____/____/____   **STEP 1**

Daily Illumination Prompt:

Today, I am deeply grateful that this person has helped me to bring light to my shadow.

[ ]

(enter the same person from your daily shadow work)

Daily Shadow Work Prompt:

Who evoked the biggest emotional response from you today? Who triggered you?

[ ]

(family member/friend/stranger/movie character etc.)

SHADOW INTEGRATION:

Below, accept & reclaim the shadow chacterter traits that had the greatest emotional impact on you from your daily shadow work AND include what the purpose or role those traits play in your life now.

(defense mechanism/self preservation etc.)

Beacuse of you, I now realize that I AM:

Describe 5 of the person's character traits:

-
-
-
-
-

Now go back and add the words "I AM" in front of each character trait above.

Which trait evoked the greatest resistance in you? Which did you feel defensive about? Allow the feelings to flow through you with self awareness of how you're feeling.

What is the oldest memory you have of when you felt that same way?
(the underlying trauma that the feelings stem from)

What would you say to your inner child if you could be there during the underyling trauma with the wisdom you have now. Show love & nurture your inner child.

STEP 3 — Cut along the dotted line, thank the person who triggered your shadow work, read out loud what you wrote in STEP 2 . Lastly release your negative resistence to your shadow by burning STEP 1

DATE _____/_____/_____   STEP 2   DATE _____/_____/_____   STEP 1

Daily Illumination Prompt:

Today, I am deeply grateful that this person has helped me to bring light to my shadow.

(enter the same person from your daily shadow work)

Daily Shadow Work Prompt:

Who evoked the biggest emotional response from you today? Who triggered you?

(family member/friend/stranger/movie character etc.)

SHADOW INTEGRATION:

Below, accept & reclaim the shadow chacterter traits that had the greatest emotional impact on you from your daily shadow work AND include what the purpose or role those traits play in your life now.
(defense mechanism/self preservation etc.)

Describe 5 of the person's character traits:

-
-
-
-
-

Beacuse of you, I now realize that I AM:

Now go back and add the words "I AM" in front of each character trait above.

Which trait evoked the greatest resistance in you? Which did you feel defensive about? Allow the feelings to flow through you with self awareness of how you're feeling.

What is the oldest memory you have of when you felt that same way?
(the underlying trauma that the feelings stem from)

What would you say to your inner child if you could be there during the underlying trauma with the wisdom you have now. Show love & nurture your inner child.

STEP 3 — Cut along the dotted line, thank the person who triggered your shadow work, read out loud what you wrote in STEP 2 . Lastly release your negative resistence to your shadow by burning STEP 1

DATE ____/____/____   STEP 2 | DATE ____/____/____   STEP 1

Daily Illumination Prompt:

Today, I am deeply grateful that this person has helped me to bring light to my shadow.

_____

(enter the same person from your daily shadow work)

Daily Shadow Work Prompt:

Who evoked the biggest emotional response from you today? Who triggered you?

_____

(family member/friend/stranger/movie character etc.)

SHADOW INTEGRATION:

Below, accept & reclaim the shadow chacterter traits that had the greatest emotional impact on you from your daily shadow work AND include what the purpose or role those traits play in your life now.

(defense mechanism/self preservation etc.)

Beacuse of you, I now realize that I AM:

Describe 5 of the person's character traits:

-
-
-
-
-

Now go back and add the words "I AM" in front of each character trait above.

Which trait evoked the greatest resistance in you? Which did you feel defensive about? Allow the feelings to flow through you with self awareness of how you're feeling.

What is the oldest memory you have of when you felt that same way?
(the underlying trauma that the feelings stem from)

What would you say to your inner child if you could be there during the underyling trauma with the wisdom you have now. Show love & nurture your inner child.

STEP 3 — Cut along the dotted line, thank the person who triggered your shadow work, read out loud what you wrote in STEP 2. Lastly release your negative resistence to your shadow by burning STEP 1

DATE ____/____/____   STEP **2** | DATE ____/____/____   STEP **1**

Daily Illumination Prompt:

Today, I am deeply grateful that this person has helped me to bring light to my shadow.

[ ]

(enter the same person from your daily shadow work)

Daily Shadow Work Prompt:

Who evoked the biggest emotional response from you today? Who triggered you?

[ ]

(family member/friend/stranger/movie character etc.)

SHADOW INTEGRATION:

Below, accept & reclaim the shadow chacterter traits that had the greatest emotional impact on you from your daily shadow work AND include what the purpose or role those traits play in your life now.
(defense mechanism/self preservation etc.)

Beacuse of you, I now realize that I AM:

Describe 5 of the person's character traits:

-
-
-
-
-

Now go back and add the words "I AM" in front of each character trait above.

Which trait evoked the greatest resistance in you? Which did you feel defensive about? Allow the feelings to flow through you with self awareness of how you're feeling.

What is the oldest memory you have of when you felt that same way?
(the underlying trauma that the feelings stem from)

What would you say to your inner child if you could be there during the underlying trauma with the wisdom you have now. Show love & nurture your inner child.

STEP **3** — Cut along the dotted line, thank the person who triggered your shadow work, read out loud what you wrote in STEP 2 . Lastly release your negative resistence to your shadow by burning STEP 1

DATE ____/____/____   **STEP 2**   DATE ____/____/____   **STEP 1**

Daily Illumination Prompt:

Today, I am deeply grateful that this person has helped me to bring light to my shadow.

(enter the same person from your daily shadow work)

Daily Shadow Work Prompt:

Who evoked the biggest emotional response from you today? Who triggered you?

(family member/friend/stranger/movie character etc.)

SHADOW INTEGRATION:

Below, accept & reclaim the shadow chacterter traits that had the greatest emotional impact on you from your daily shadow work AND include what the purpose or role those traits play in your life now.

(defense mechanism/self preservation etc.)

Beacuse of you, I now realize that I AM:

Describe 5 of the person's character traits:

-
-
-
-
-

Now go back and add the words "I AM" in front of each character trait above.

Which trait evoked the greatest resistance in you? Which did you feel defensive about? Allow the feelings to flow through you with self awareness of how you're feeling.

What is the oldest memory you have of when you felt that same way?
(the underlying trauma that the feelings stem from)

What would you say to your inner child if you could be there during the underyling trauma with the wisdom you have now. Show love & nurture your inner child.

STEP 3 — Cut along the dotted line, thank the person who triggered your shadow work, read out loud what you wrote in STEP 2 . Lastly release your negative resistence to your shadow by burning STEP 1

DATE _____/_____/_____   STEP **2** | DATE _____/_____/_____   STEP **1**

Daily Illumination Prompt:

Today, I am deeply grateful that this person has helped me to bring light to my shadow.

[ ]

(enter the same person from your daily shadow work)

Daily Shadow Work Prompt:

Who evoked the biggest emotional response from you today? Who triggered you?

[ ]

(family member/friend/stranger/movie character etc.)

SHADOW INTEGRATION:

Below, accept & reclaim the shadow chacterter traits that had the greatest emotional impact on you from your daily shadow work AND include what the purpose or role those traits play in your life now.

(defense mechanism/self preservation etc.)

Beacuse of you, I now realize that I AM:

Describe 5 of the person's character traits:

- -
- -
- -
- -
- -

Now go back and add the words "I AM" in front of each character trait above.

Which trait evoked the greatest resistance in you? Which did you feel defensive about? Allow the feelings to flow through you with self awareness of how you're feeling.

What is the oldest memory you have of when you felt that same way?
(the underlying trauma that the feelings stem from)

What would you say to your inner child if you could be there during the underyling trauma with the wisdom you have now. Show love & nurture your inner child.

STEP **3** — Cut along the dotted line, thank the person who triggered your shadow work, read out loud what you wrote in STEP 2 . Lastly release your negative resistence to your shadow by burning STEP 1

DATE ____/____/____   **STEP** 2

Daily Illumination Prompt:

Today, I am deeply grateful that this person has helped me to bring light to my shadow.

[ ]

(enter the same person from your daily shadow work)

SHADOW INTEGRATION:

Below, accept & reclaim the shadow chacterter traits that had the greatest emotional impact on you from your daily shadow work AND include what the purpose or role those traits play in your life now.

(defense mechanism/self preservation etc.)

Beacuse of you, I now realize that I AM:

DATE ____/____/____   **STEP** 1

Daily Shadow Work Prompt:

Who evoked the biggest emotional response from you today? Who triggered you?

[ ]

(family member/friend/stranger/movie character etc.)

Describe 5 of the person's character traits:

-
-
-
-
-

Now go back and add the words "I AM" in front of each character trait above.

Which trait evoked the greatest resistance in you? Which did you feel defensive about? Allow the feelings to flow through you with self awareness of how you're feeling.

What is the oldest memory you have of when you felt that same way?
(the underlying trauma that the feelings stem from)

What would you say to your inner child if you could be there during the underyling trauma with the wisdom you have now. Show love & nurture your inner child.

STEP 3 – Cut along the dotted line, thank the person who triggered your shadow work, read out loud what you wrote in STEP 2 . Lastly release your negative resistence to your shadow by burning STEP 1

Daily Illumination Prompt:

Today, I am deeply grateful that this person has helped me to bring light to my shadow.

[ ]

(enter the same person from your daily shadow work)

SHADOW INTEGRATION:

Below, accept & reclaim the shadow chacterter traits that had the greatest emotional impact on you from your daily shadow work AND include what the purpose or role those traits play in your life now.
(defense mechanism/self preservation etc.)

Beacuse of you, I now realize that I AM:

Daily Shadow Work Prompt:

Who evoked the biggest emotional response from you today? Who triggered you?

[ ]

(family member/friend/stranger/movie character etc.)

Describe 5 of the person's character traits:

-
-
-
-
-

Now go back and add the words "I AM" in front of each character trait above.

Which trait evoked the greatest resistance in you? Which did you feel defensive about? Allow the feelings to flow through you with self awareness of how you're feeling.

What is the oldest memory you have of when you felt that same way?
(the underlying trauma that the feelings stem from)

What would you say to your inner child if you could be there during the underyling trauma with the wisdom you have now. Show love & nurture your inner child.

STEP 3 — Cut along the dotted line, thank the person who triggered your shadow work, read out loud what you wrote in STEP 2 . Lastly release your negative resistence to your shadow by burning STEP 1

DATE ____/____/____　　　　　　**STEP** 2 ┊ DATE ____/____/____　　　　　　**STEP** 1

Daily Illumination Prompt:

Today, I am deeply grateful that this person has helped me to bring light to my shadow.

[ ]

(enter the same person from your daily shadow work)

Daily Shadow Work Prompt:

Who evoked the biggest emotional response from you today? Who triggered you?

[ ]

(family member/friend/stranger/movie character etc.)

SHADOW INTEGRATION:

Below, accept & reclaim the shadow chacterter traits that had the greatest emotional impact on you from your daily shadow work AND include what the purpose or role those traits play in your life now.
(defense mechanism/self preservation etc.)

Beacuse of you, I now realize that I AM:

Describe 5 of the person's character traits:

-
-
-
-
-

Now go back and add the words "I AM" in front of each character trait above.

Which trait evoked the greatest resistance in you? Which did you feel defensive about? Allow the feelings to flow through you with self awareness of how you're feeling.

What is the oldest memory you have of when you felt that same way?
(the underlying trauma that the feelings stem from)

What would you say to your inner child if you could be there during the underlying trauma with the wisdom you have now. Show love & nurture your inner child.

— Cut along the dotted line, thank the person who triggered your shadow work, read out loud what you wrote in STEP 2. Lastly release your negative resistence to your shadow by burning STEP 1

STEP 3

DATE ____/____/____   STEP 2 | DATE ____/____/____   STEP 1

Daily Illumination Prompt:

Today, I am deeply grateful that this person has helped me to bring light to my shadow.

[ ]

(enter the same person from your daily shadow work)

Daily Shadow Work Prompt:

Who evoked the biggest emotional response from you today? Who triggered you?

[ ]

(family member/friend/stranger/movie character etc.)

SHADOW INTEGRATION:

Below, accept & reclaim the shadow chacterter traits that had the greatest emotional impact on you from your daily shadow work AND include what the purpose or role those traits play in your life now.

(defense mechanism/self preservation etc.)

Beacuse of you, I now realize that I AM:

Describe 5 of the person's character traits:

-

-

-

-

-

Now go back and add the words "I AM" in front of each character trait above.

Which trait evoked the greatest resistance in you? Which did you feel defensive about? Allow the feelings to flow through you with self awareness of how you're feeling.

What is the oldest memory you have of when you felt that same way?
(the underlying trauma that the feelings stem from)

What would you say to your inner child if you could be there during the underlying trauma with the wisdom you have now. Show love & nurture your inner child.

STEP 3 — Cut along the dotted line, thank the person who triggered your shadow work, read out loud what you wrote in STEP 2 . Lastly release your negative resistence to your shadow by burning STEP 1

DATE ____/____/____   STEP 2 │ DATE ____/____/____   STEP 1

Daily Illumination Prompt:

Today, I am deeply grateful that this person has helped me to bring light to my shadow.

[   ]

(enter the same person from your daily shadow work)

│

Daily Shadow Work Prompt:

Who evoked the biggest emotional response from you today? Who triggered you?

[   ]

(family member/friend/stranger/movie character etc.)

SHADOW INTEGRATION:

Below, accept & reclaim the shadow chacterter traits that had the greatest emotional impact on you from your daily shadow work AND include what the purpose or role those traits play in your life now.

(defense mechanism/self preservation etc.)

Beacuse of you, I now realize that I AM:

│

Describe 5 of the person's character traits:

-
-
-
-
-

Now go back and add the words "I AM" in front of each character trait above.

Which trait evoked the greatest resistance in you? Which did you feel defensive about? Allow the feelings to flow through you with self awareness of how you're feeling.

What is the oldest memory you have of when you felt that same way?
(the underlying trauma that the feelings stem from)

What would you say to your inner child if you could be there during the underlying trauma with the wisdom you have now. Show love & nurture your inner child.

STEP 3 — Cut along the dotted line, thank the person who triggered your shadow work, read out loud what you wrote in STEP 2 . Lastly release your negative resistence to your shadow by burning STEP 1

DATE ____/____/____   STEP **2** | DATE ____/____/____   STEP **1**

Daily Illumination Prompt:

Today, I am deeply grateful that this person has helped me to bring light to my shadow.

[ ]

(enter the same person from your daily shadow work)

Daily Shadow Work Prompt:

Who evoked the biggest emotional response from you today? Who triggered you?

[ ]

(family member/friend/stranger/movie character etc.)

SHADOW INTEGRATION:

Below, accept & reclaim the shadow chacterter traits that had the greatest emotional impact on you from your daily shadow work AND include what the purpose or role those traits play in your life now.

(defense mechanism/self preservation etc.)

Beacuse of you, I now realize that I AM:

Describe 5 of the person's character traits:

-
-
-
-
-

Now go back and add the words "I AM" in front of each character trait above.

Which trait evoked the greatest resistance in you? Which did you feel defensive about? Allow the feelings to flow through you with self awareness of how you're feeling.

What is the oldest memory you have of when you felt that same way?
(the underlying trauma that the feelings stem from)

What would you say to your inner child if you could be there during the underyling trauma with the wisdom you have now. Show love & nurture your inner child.

STEP **3** — Cut along the dotted line, thank the person who triggered your shadow work, read out loud what you wrote in STEP 2 . Lastly release your negative resistence to your shadow by burning STEP 1

DATE ___ / ___ / ___   STEP **2** | DATE ___ / ___ / ___   STEP **1**

Daily Illumination Prompt:

Today, I am deeply grateful that this person has helped me to bring light to my shadow.

[ ]

(enter the same person from your daily shadow work)

Daily Shadow Work Prompt:

Who evoked the biggest emotional response from you today? Who triggered you?

[ ]

(family member/friend/stranger/movie character etc.)

SHADOW INTEGRATION:

Below, accept & reclaim the shadow chacterter traits that had the greatest emotional impact on you from your daily shadow work AND include what the purpose or role those traits play in your life now.

(defense mechanism/self preservation etc.)

Beacuse of you, I now realize that I AM:

Describe 5 of the person's character traits:

-
-
-
-
-

Now go back and add the words "I AM" in front of each character trait above.

Which trait evoked the greatest resistance in you? Which did you feel defensive about? Allow the feelings to flow through you with self awareness of how you're feeling.

What is the oldest memory you have of when you felt that same way?
(the underlying trauma that the feelings stem from)

What would you say to your inner child if you could be there during the underyling trauma with the wisdom you have now. Show love & nurture your inner child.

STEP **3** - Cut along the dotted line, thank the person who triggered your shadow work, read out loud what you wrote in STEP 2 . Lastly release your negative resistence to your shadow by burning STEP 1

DATE _____/_____/_____   STEP **2**   DATE _____/_____/_____   STEP **1**

Daily Illumination Prompt:

Today, I am deeply grateful that this person has helped me to bring light to my shadow.

[ ]

(enter the same person from your daily shadow work)

Daily Shadow Work Prompt:

Who evoked the biggest emotional response from you today? Who triggered you?

[ ]

(family member/friend/stranger/movie character etc.)

SHADOW INTEGRATION:

Below, accept & reclaim the shadow chacterter traits that had the greatest emotional impact on you from your daily shadow work AND include what the purpose or role those traits play in your life now.

(defense mechanism/self preservation etc.)

Beacuse of you, I now realize that I AM:

Describe 5 of the person's character traits:

-
-
-
-
-

Now go back and add the words "I AM" in front of each character trait above.

Which trait evoked the greatest resistance in you? Which did you feel defensive about? Allow the feelings to flow through you with self awareness of how you're feeling.

What is the oldest memory you have of when you felt that same way?
(the underlying trauma that the feelings stem from)

What would you say to your inner child if you could be there during the underyling trauma with the wisdom you have now. Show love & nurture your inner child.

STEP **3** — Cut along the dotted line, thank the person who triggered your shadow work, read out loud what you wrote in STEP 2 . Lastly release your negative resistence to your shadow by burning STEP 1

DATE ____/____/____   **STEP 2**   DATE ____/____/____   **STEP 1**

Daily Illumination Prompt:

Today, I am deeply grateful that this person has helped me to bring light to my shadow.

[   ]

(enter the same person from your daily shadow work)

Daily Shadow Work Prompt:

Who evoked the biggest emotional response from you today? Who triggered you?

[   ]

(family member/friend/stranger/movie character etc.)

SHADOW INTEGRATION:

Below, accept & reclaim the shadow chacterter traits that had the greatest emotional impact on you from your daily shadow work AND include what the purpose or role those traits play in your life now.

(defense mechanism/self preservation etc.)

Beacuse of you, I now realize that I AM:

Describe 5 of the person's character traits:

-
-
-
-
-

Now go back and add the words "I AM" in front of each character trait above.

Which trait evoked the greatest resistance in you? Which did you feel defensive about? Allow the feelings to flow through you with self awareness of how you're feeling.

What is the oldest memory you have of when you felt that same way?
(the underlying trauma that the feelings stem from)

What would you say to your inner child if you could be there during the underlying trauma with the wisdom you have now. Show love & nurture your inner child.

STEP 3 — Cut along the dotted line, thank the person who triggered your shadow work, read out loud what you wrote in STEP 2 . Lastly release your negative resistence to your shadow by burning STEP 1

DATE ____/____/____   STEP **2**   DATE ____/____/____   STEP 1

Daily Illumination Prompt:

Today, I am deeply grateful that this person has helped me to bring light to my shadow.

[ ]

(enter the same person from your daily shadow work)

Daily Shadow Work Prompt:

Who evoked the biggest emotional response from you today? Who triggered you?

[ ]

(family member/friend/stranger/movie character etc.)

SHADOW INTEGRATION:

Below, accept & reclaim the shadow chacterter traits that had the greatest emotional impact on you from your daily shadow work AND include what the purpose or role those traits play in your life now.
(defense mechanism/self preservation etc.)

Beacuse of you, I now realize that I AM:

Describe 5 of the person's character traits:

-
-
-
-
-

Now go back and add the words "I AM" in front of each character trait above.

Which trait evoked the greatest resistance in you? Which did you feel defensive about? Allow the feelings to flow through you with self awareness of how you're feeling.

What is the oldest memory you have of when you felt that same way?
(the underlying trauma that the feelings stem from)

What would you say to your inner child if you could be there during the underyling trauma with the wisdom you have now. Show love & nurture your inner child.

STEP 3 — Cut along the dotted line, thank the person who triggered your shadow work, read out loud what you wrote in STEP 2 . Lastly release your negative resistence to your shadow by burning STEP 1

DATE _____/_____/_____   STEP 2

Daily Illumination Prompt:

Today, I am deeply grateful that this person has helped me to bring light to my shadow.

```
[                                    ]
```

(enter the same person from your daily shadow work)

SHADOW INTEGRATION:

Below, accept & reclaim the shadow chacterter traits that had the greatest emotional impact on you from your daily shadow work AND include what the purpose or role those traits play in your life now.
(defense mechanism/self preservation etc.)

Beacuse of you, I now realize that I AM:

DATE _____/_____/_____   STEP 1

Daily Shadow Work Prompt:

Who evoked the biggest emotional response from you today? Who triggered you?

```
[                                    ]
```

(family member/friend/stranger/movie character etc.)

Describe 5 of the person's character traits:

-
-
-
-
-

Now go back and add the words "I AM" in front of each character trait above.

Which trait evoked the greatest resistence in you? Which did you feel defensive about? Allow the feelings to flow through you with self awareness of how you're feeling.

What is the oldest memory you have of when you felt that same way?
(the underlying trauma that the feelings stem from)

What would you say to your inner child if you could be there during the underyling trauma with the wisdom you have now. Show love & nurture your inner child.

STEP 3 — Cut along the dotted line, thank the person who triggered your shadow work, read out loud what you wrote in STEP 2 . Lastly release your negative resistence to your shadow by burning STEP 1

Daily Illumination Prompt:

Today, I am deeply grateful that this person has helped me to bring light to my shadow.

(enter the same person from your daily shadow work)

Daily Shadow Work Prompt:

Who evoked the biggest emotional response from you today? Who triggered you?

(family member/friend/stranger/movie character etc.)

SHADOW INTEGRATION:

Below, accept & reclaim the shadow chacterter traits that had the greatest emotional impact on you from your daily shadow work AND include what the purpose or role those traits play in your life now.

(defense mechanism/self preservation etc.)

Beacuse of you, I now realize that I AM:

Describe 5 of the person's character traits:

-
-
-
-
-

Now go back and add the words "I AM" in front of each character trait above.

Which trait evoked the greatest resistance in you? Which did you feel defensive about? Allow the feelings to flow through you with self awareness of how you're feeling.

What is the oldest memory you have of when you felt that same way?
(the underlying trauma that the feelings stem from)

What would you say to your inner child if you could be there during the underlying trauma with the wisdom you have now. Show love & nurture your inner child.

STEP 3 — Cut along the dotted line, thank the person who triggered your shadow work, read out loud what you wrote in STEP 2 . Lastly release your negative resistence to your shadow by burning STEP 1

DATE ____/____/____   STEP 2 | DATE ____/____/____   STEP 1

Daily Illumination Prompt:

Today, I am deeply grateful that this person has helped me to bring light to my shadow.

[ ]

(enter the same person from your daily shadow work)

| ## Daily Shadow Work Prompt:

Who evoked the biggest emotional response from you today? Who triggered you?

[ ]

(family member/friend/stranger/movie character etc.)

SHADOW INTEGRATION:

Below, accept & reclaim the shadow chacterter traits that had the greatest emotional impact on you from your daily shadow work AND include what the purpose or role those traits play in your life now.
(defense mechanism/self preservation etc.)

Beacuse of you, I now realize that I AM:

| *Describe 5 of the person's character traits:*

-
-
-
-
-

Now go back and add the words "I AM" in front of each character trait above.

Which trait evoked the greatest resistance in you? Which did you feel defensive about? Allow the feelings to flow through you with self awareness of how you're feeling.

What is the oldest memory you have of when you felt that same way?
(the underlying trauma that the feelings stem from)

What would you say to your inner child if you could be there during the underlying trauma with the wisdom you have now. Show love & nurture your inner child.

STEP 3 — Cut along the dotted line, thank the person who triggered your shadow work, read out loud what you wrote in STEP 2. Lastly release your negative resistence to your shadow by burning STEP 1

DATE ____/____/____ **STEP 2** | DATE ____/____/____ **STEP 1**

Daily Illumination Prompt:

Today, I am deeply grateful that this person has helped me to bring light to my shadow.

> [ ]

(enter the same person from your daily shadow work)

Daily Shadow Work Prompt:

Who evoked the biggest emotional response from you today? Who triggered you?

> [ ]

(family member/friend/stranger/movie character etc.)

SHADOW INTEGRATION:

Below, accept & reclaim the shadow chacterter traits that had the greatest emotional impact on you from your daily shadow work AND include what the purpose or role those traits play in your life now.

(defense mechanism/self preservation etc.)

Beacuse of you, I now realize that I AM:

Describe 5 of the person's character traits:

-
-
-
-
-

Now go back and add the words "I AM" in front of each character trait above.

Which trait evoked the greatest resistance in you? Which did you feel defensive about? Allow the feelings to flow through you with self awareness of how you're feeling.

What is the oldest memory you have of when you felt that same way?
(the underlying trauma that the feelings stem from)

What would you say to your inner child if you could be there during the underyling trauma with the wisdom you have now. Show love & nurture your inner child.

STEP 3 — Cut along the dotted line, thank the person who triggered your shadow work, read out loud what you wrote in STEP 2 . Lastly release your negative resistence to your shadow by burning STEP 1

DATE _____/_____/_____   STEP **2**

Daily Illumination Prompt:

Today, I am deeply grateful that this person has helped me to bring light to my shadow.

[   ]

(enter the same person from your daily shadow work)

SHADOW INTEGRATION:

Below, accept & reclaim the shadow chacterter traits that had the greatest emotional impact on you from your daily shadow work AND include what the purpose or role those traits play in your life now.

(defense mechanism/self preservation etc.)

Beacuse of you, I now realize that I AM:

DATE _____/_____/_____   STEP **1**

Daily Shadow Work Prompt:

Who evoked the biggest emotional response from you today? Who triggered you?

[   ]

(family member/friend/stranger/movie character etc.)

Describe 5 of the person's character traits:

-
-
-
-
-

Now go back and add the words "I AM" in front of each character trait above.

Which trait evoked the greatest resistance in you? Which did you feel defensive about? Allow the feelings to flow through you with self awareness of how you're feeling.

What is the oldest memory you have of when you felt that same way?
(the underlying trauma that the feelings stem from)

What would you say to your inner child if you could be there during the underlying trauma with the wisdom you have now. Show love & nurture your inner child.

STEP **3** — Cut along the dotted line, thank the person who triggered your shadow work, read out loud what you wrote in STEP 2 . Lastly release your negative resistence to your shadow by burning STEP 1

Daily Illumination Prompt:

Today, I am deeply grateful that this person has helped me to bring light to my shadow.

(enter the same person from your daily shadow work)

Daily Shadow Work Prompt:

Who evoked the biggest emotional response from you today? Who triggered you?

(family member/friend/stranger/movie character etc.)

SHADOW INTEGRATION:

Below, accept & reclaim the shadow chacterter traits that had the greatest emotional impact on you from your daily shadow work AND include what the purpose or role those traits play in your life now.

(defense mechanism/self preservation etc.)

Beacuse of you, I now realize that I AM:

Describe 5 of the person's character traits:

-
-
-
-
-

Now go back and add the words "I AM" in front of each character trait above.

Which trait evoked the greatest resistance in you? Which did you feel defensive about? Allow the feelings to flow through you with self awareness of how you're feeling.

What is the oldest memory you have of when you felt that same way?
(the underlying trauma that the feelings stem from)

What would you say to your inner child if you could be there during the underlying trauma with the wisdom you have now. Show love & nurture your inner child.

STEP 3 — Cut along the dotted line, thank the person who triggered your shadow work, read out loud what you wrote in STEP 2 . Lastly release your negative resistence to your shadow by burning STEP 1

DATE ____/____/____   **STEP 2**

Daily Illumination Prompt:

Today, I am deeply grateful that this person has helped me to bring light to my shadow.

[   ]

(enter the same person from your daily shadow work)

SHADOW INTEGRATION:

Below, accept & reclaim the shadow chacterter traits that had the greatest emotional impact on you from your daily shadow work AND include what the purpose or role those traits play in your life now.
(defense mechanism/self preservation etc.)

Beacuse of you, I now realize that I AM:

DATE ____/____/____   **STEP 1**

Daily Shadow Work Prompt:

Who evoked the biggest emotional response from you today? Who triggered you?

[   ]

(family member/friend/stranger/movie character etc.)

Describe 5 of the person's character traits:

-
-
-
-
-

Now go back and add the words "I AM" in front of each character trait above.

Which trait evoked the greatest resistance in you? Which did you feel defensive about? Allow the feelings to flow through you with self awareness of how you're feeling.

What is the oldest memory you have of when you felt that same way?
(the underlying trauma that the feelings stem from)

What would you say to your inner child if you could be there during the underyling trauma with the wisdom you have now. Show love & nurture your inner child.

Cut along the dotted line, thank the person who triggered your shadow work, read out loud what you wrote in STEP 2. Lastly release your negative resistence to your shadow by burning STEP 1

STEP 3

DATE ____/____/____   **STEP** 2   DATE ____/____/____   **STEP** 1

Daily Illumination Prompt:

Today, I am deeply grateful that this person has helped me to bring light to my shadow.

[ ]

(enter the same person from your daily shadow work)

Daily Shadow Work Prompt:

Who evoked the biggest emotional response from you today? Who triggered you?

[ ]

(family member/friend/stranger/movie character etc.)

SHADOW INTEGRATION:

Below, accept & reclaim the shadow chacterter traits that had the greatest emotional impact on you from your daily shadow work AND include what the purpose or role those traits play in your life now.

(defense mechanism/self preservation etc.)

Beacuse of you, I now realize that I AM:

Describe 5 of the person's character traits:

-
-
-
-
-

Now go back and add the words "I AM" in front of each character trait above.

Which trait evoked the greatest resistence in you? Which did you feel defensive about? Allow the feelings to flow through you with self awareness of how you're feeling.

What is the oldest memory you have of when you felt that same way?
(the underlying trauma that the feelings stem from)

What would you say to your inner child if you could be there during the underyling trauma with the wisdom you have now. Show love & nurture your inner child.

– Cut along the dotted line, thank the person who triggered your shadow work, read out loud what you wrote in STEP 2 . Lastly release your negative resistence to your shadow by burning STEP 1

STEP 3

STEP 3

DATE ___ / ___ / ___   **STEP** 2 | DATE ___ / ___ / ___   **STEP** 1

Daily Illumination Prompt:

Today, I am deeply grateful that this person has helped me to bring light to my shadow.

┌─────────────────────────────────────┐
│   │
└─────────────────────────────────────┘

(enter the same person from your daily shadow work)

Daily Shadow Work Prompt:

Who evoked the biggest emotional response from you today? Who triggered you?

┌─────────────────────────────────────┐
│   │
└─────────────────────────────────────┘

(family member/friend/stranger/movie character etc.)

SHADOW INTEGRATION:

Below, accept & reclaim the shadow chacterter traits that had the greatest emotional impact on you from your daily shadow work AND include what the purpose or role those traits play in your life now.
(defense mechanism/self preservation etc.)

Beacuse of you, I now realize that I AM:

Describe 5 of the person's character traits:

-
-
-
-
-

Now go back and add the words "I AM" in front of each character trait above.

Which trait evoked the greatest resistance in you? Which did you feel defensive about? Allow the feelings to flow through you with self awareness of how you're feeling.

What is the oldest memory you have of when you felt that same way?
(the underlying trauma that the feelings stem from)

What would you say to your inner child if you could be there during the underyling trauma with the wisdom you have now. Show love & nurture your inner child.

STEP 3 — Cut along the dotted line, thank the person who triggered your shadow work, read out loud what you wrote in STEP 2 . Lastly release your negative resistence to your shadow by burning STEP 1

DATE ___/___/___   **STEP** 2 | DATE ___/___/___   **STEP** 1

Daily Illumination Prompt:

*Today, I am deeply grateful that this person
has helped me to bring light to my shadow.*

[ ]

(enter the same person from your daily shadow work)

Daily Shadow Work Prompt:

*Who evoked the biggest emotional response
from you today? Who triggered you?*

[ ]

(family member/friend/stranger/movie character etc.)

SHADOW INTEGRATION:

**Below, accept & reclaim the shadow
chacterter traits that had the greatest
emotional impact on you from your daily
shadow work AND include what the
purpose or role those traits play in your
life now.**

(defense mechanism/self preservation etc.)

Beacuse of you, I now realize that I AM:

Describe 5 of the person's character traits:

-
-
-
-
-

**Now go back and add the words "I AM" in
front of each character trait above.**

*Which trait evoked the greatest resistance
in you? Which did you feel defensive about?
Allow the feelings to flow through you with
self awareness of how you're feeling.*

*What is the oldest memory you have of
when you felt that same way?*
(the underlying trauma that the feelings stem from)

*What would you say to your inner child if
you could be there during the underyling
trauma with the wisdom you have now.
Show love & nurture your inner child.*

STEP 3 — Cut along the dotted line, thank the person who triggered your shadow work, read out loud what you wrote in STEP 2. Lastly release your negative resistence to your shadow by burning STEP 1

DATE ____/____/____ **STEP** 2

Daily Illumination Prompt:

Today, I am deeply grateful that this person has helped me to bring light to my shadow.

[ ]

(enter the same person from your daily shadow work)

SHADOW INTEGRATION:

Below, accept & reclaim the shadow chacterter traits that had the greatest emotional impact on you from your daily shadow work AND include what the purpose or role those traits play in your life now.
(defense mechanism/self preservation etc.)

Beacuse of you, I now realize that I AM:

DATE ____/____/____ **STEP** 1

Daily Shadow Work Prompt:

Who evoked the biggest emotional response from you today? Who triggered you?

[ ]

(family member/friend/stranger/movie character etc.)

Describe 5 of the person's character traits:

-
-
-
-
-

Now go back and add the words "I AM" in front of each character trait above.

Which trait evoked the greatest resistance in you? Which did you feel defensive about? Allow the feelings to flow through you with self awareness of how you're feeling.

What is the oldest memory you have of when you felt that same way?
(the underlying trauma that the feelings stem from)

What would you say to your inner child if you could be there during the underyling trauma with the wisdom you have now. Show love & nurture your inner child.

STEP 3 – Cut along the dotted line, thank the person who triggered your shadow work, read out loud what you wrote in STEP 2 . Lastly release your negative resistence to your shadow by burning STEP 1

DATE ____/____/____   **STEP 2** | DATE ____/____/____   **STEP 1**

Daily Illumination Prompt:	**Daily Shadow Work Prompt:**
Today, I am deeply grateful that this person has helped me to bring light to my shadow.	*Who evoked the biggest emotional response from you today? Who triggered you?*
(enter the same person from your daily shadow work)	*(family member/friend/stranger/movie character etc.)*

SHADOW INTEGRATION:

Below, accept & reclaim the shadow chacterter traits that had the greatest emotional impact on you from your daily shadow work AND include what the purpose or role those traits play in your life now.
(defense mechanism/self preservation etc.)

Beacuse of you, I now realize that I AM:

Describe 5 of the person's character traits:

-
-
-
-
-

Now go back and add the words "I AM" in front of each character trait above.

Which trait evoked the greatest resistance in you? Which did you feel defensive about? Allow the feelings to flow through you with self awareness of how you're feeling.

What is the oldest memory you have of when you felt that same way?
(the underlying trauma that the feelings stem from)

What would you say to your inner child if you could be there during the underlying trauma with the wisdom you have now. Show love & nurture your inner child.

STEP 3 — Cut along the dotted line, thank the person who triggered your shadow work, read out loud what you wrote in STEP 2 . Lastly release your negative resistence to your shadow by burning STEP 1

Daily Illumination Prompt:

Today, I am deeply grateful that this person has helped me to bring light to my shadow.

(enter the same person from your daily shadow work)

Daily Shadow Work Prompt:

Who evoked the biggest emotional response from you today? Who triggered you?

(family member/friend/stranger/movie character etc.)

SHADOW INTEGRATION:

Below, accept & reclaim the shadow chacterter traits that had the greatest emotional impact on you from your daily shadow work AND include what the purpose or role those traits play in your life now.

(defense mechanism/self preservation etc.)

Beacuse of you, I now realize that I AM:

Describe 5 of the person's character traits:

-
-
-
-
-

Now go back and add the words "I AM" in front of each character trait above.

Which trait evoked the greatest resistance in you? Which did you feel defensive about? Allow the feelings to flow through you with self awareness of how you're feeling.

What is the oldest memory you have of when you felt that same way?
(the underlying trauma that the feelings stem from)

What would you say to your inner child if you could be there during the underyling trauma with the wisdom you have now. Show love & nurture your inner child.

STEP 3 — Cut along the dotted line, thank the person who triggered your shadow work, read out loud what you wrote in STEP 2 . Lastly release your negative resistence to your shadow by burning STEP 1

Daily Illumination Prompt:

Today, I am deeply grateful that this person has helped me to bring light to my shadow.

(enter the same person from your daily shadow work)

Daily Shadow Work Prompt:

Who evoked the biggest emotional response from you today? Who triggered you?

(family member/friend/stranger/movie character etc.)

SHADOW INTEGRATION:

Below, accept & reclaim the shadow chacterter traits that had the greatest emotional impact on you from your daily shadow work AND include what the purpose or role those traits play in your life now.

(defense mechanism/self preservation etc.)

Beacuse of you, I now realize that I AM:

Describe 5 of the person's character traits:

-
-
-
-
-

Now go back and add the words "I AM" in front of each character trait above.

Which trait evoked the greatest resistance in you? Which did you feel defensive about? Allow the feelings to flow through you with self awareness of how you're feeling.

What is the oldest memory you have of when you felt that same way?
(the underlying trauma that the feelings stem from)

What would you say to your inner child if you could be there during the underlying trauma with the wisdom you have now. Show love & nurture your inner child.

STEP 3 — Cut along the dotted line, thank the person who triggered your shadow work, read out loud what you wrote in STEP 2 . Lastly release your negative resistence to your shadow by burning STEP 1

DATE ____/____/____   STEP 2   DATE ____/____/____   STEP 1

Daily Illumination Prompt:

Today, I am deeply grateful that this person has helped me to bring light to my shadow.

[   ]

(enter the same person from your daily shadow work)

Daily Shadow Work Prompt:

Who evoked the biggest emotional response from you today? Who triggered you?

[   ]

(family member/friend/stranger/movie character etc.)

SHADOW INTEGRATION:

Below, accept & reclaim the shadow chacterter traits that had the greatest emotional impact on you from your daily shadow work AND include what the purpose or role those traits play in your life now.

(defense mechanism/self preservation etc.)

Beacuse of you, I now realize that I AM:

Describe 5 of the person's character traits:

-
-
-
-
-

Now go back and add the words "I AM" in front of each character trait above.

Which trait evoked the greatest resistance in you? Which did you feel defensive about? Allow the feelings to flow through you with self awareness of how you're feeling.

What is the oldest memory you have of when you felt that same way?
(the underlying trauma that the feelings stem from)

What would you say to your inner child if you could be there during the underyling trauma with the wisdom you have now. Show love & nurture your inner child.

STEP 3 — Cut along the dotted line, thank the person who triggered your shadow work, read out loud what you wrote in STEP 2 . Lastly release your negative resistence to your shadow by burning STEP 1

Daily Illumination Prompt:

Today, I am deeply grateful that this person has helped me to bring light to my shadow.

(enter the same person from your daily shadow work)

Daily Shadow Work Prompt:

Who evoked the biggest emotional response from you today? Who triggered you?

(family member/friend/stranger/movie character etc.)

SHADOW INTEGRATION:

Below, accept & reclaim the shadow chacterter traits that had the greatest emotional impact on you from your daily shadow work AND include what the purpose or role those traits play in your life now.
(defense mechanism/self preservation etc.)

Beacuse of you, I now realize that I AM:

Describe 5 of the person's character traits:

-
-
-
-
-

Now go back and add the words "I AM" in front of each character trait above.

Which trait evoked the greatest resistance in you? Which did you feel defensive about? Allow the feelings to flow through you with self awareness of how you're feeling.

What is the oldest memory you have of when you felt that same way?
(the underlying trauma that the feelings stem from)

What would you say to your inner child if you could be there during the underyling trauma with the wisdom you have now. Show love & nurture your inner child.

DATE ____/____/____   **STEP 2**

Daily Illumination Prompt:

Today, I am deeply grateful that this person has helped me to bring light to my shadow.

```
┌─────────────────────────────────┐
│                                 │
│                                 │
└─────────────────────────────────┘
```

(enter the same person from your daily shadow work)

SHADOW INTEGRATION:

Below, accept & reclaim the shadow chacterter traits that had the greatest emotional impact on you from your daily shadow work AND include what the purpose or role those traits play in your life now.

(defense mechanism/self preservation etc.)

Beacuse of you, I now realize that I AM:

DATE ____/____/____   **STEP 1**

Daily Shadow Work Prompt:

Who evoked the biggest emotional response from you today? Who triggered you?

```
┌─────────────────────────────────┐
│                                 │
│                                 │
└─────────────────────────────────┘
```

(family member/friend/stranger/movie character etc.)

Describe 5 of the person's character traits:

-
-
-
-
-

Now go back and add the words "I AM" in front of each character trait above.

Which trait evoked the greatest resistance in you? Which did you feel defensive about? Allow the feelings to flow through you with self awareness of how you're feeling.

What is the oldest memory you have of when you felt that same way?
(the underlying trauma that the feelings stem from)

What would you say to your inner child if you could be there during the underyling trauma with the wisdom you have now. Show love & nurture your inner child.

STEP 3 — Cut along the dotted line, thank the person who triggered your shadow work, read out loud what you wrote in STEP 2 . Lastly release your negative resistence to your shadow by burning STEP 1

Daily Illumination Prompt:

Today, I am deeply grateful that this person has helped me to bring light to my shadow.

```
[                                    ]
```

(enter the same person from your daily shadow work)

SHADOW INTEGRATION:

Below, accept & reclaim the shadow chacterter traits that had the greatest emotional impact on you from your daily shadow work AND include what the purpose or role those traits play in your life now.

(defense mechanism/self preservation etc.)

Beacuse of you, I now realize that I AM:

– Cut along the dotted line, thank the person who triggered your shadow work, read out loud what you wrote in STEP 2 . Lastly release your negative resistence to your shadow by burning STEP 1

Daily Shadow Work Prompt:

Who evoked the biggest emotional response from you today? Who triggered you?

```
[                                    ]
```

(family member/friend/stranger/movie character etc.)

Describe 5 of the person's character traits:

-
-
-
-
-

Now go back and add the words "I AM" in front of each character trait above.

Which trait evoked the greatest resistance in you? Which did you feel defensive about? Allow the feelings to flow through you with self awareness of how you're feeling.

What is the oldest memory you have of when you felt that same way?
(the underlying trauma that the feelings stem from)

What would you say to your inner child if you could be there during the underyling trauma with the wisdom you have now. Show love & nurture your inner child.

Daily Illumination Prompt:

Today, I am deeply grateful that this person has helped me to bring light to my shadow.

(enter the same person from your daily shadow work)

Daily Shadow Work Prompt:

Who evoked the biggest emotional response from you today? Who triggered you?

(family member/friend/stranger/movie character etc.)

SHADOW INTEGRATION:

Below, accept & reclaim the shadow chacterter traits that had the greatest emotional impact on you from your daily shadow work AND include what the purpose or role those traits play in your life now.
(defense mechanism/self preservation etc.)

Beacuse of you, I now realize that I AM:

Describe 5 of the person's character traits:

-
-
-
-
-

Now go back and add the words "I AM" in front of each character trait above.

Which trait evoked the greatest resistance in you? Which did you feel defensive about? Allow the feelings to flow through you with self awareness of how you're feeling.

What is the oldest memory you have of when you felt that same way?
(the underlying trauma that the feelings stem from)

What would you say to your inner child if you could be there during the underyling trauma with the wisdom you have now. Show love & nurture your inner child.

STEP 3 — Cut along the dotted line, thank the person who triggered your shadow work, read out loud what you wrote in STEP 2 . Lastly release your negative resistence to your shadow by burning STEP 1

DATE ____/____/____   **STEP** 2

Daily Illumination Prompt:

Today, I am deeply grateful that this person has helped me to bring light to my shadow.

[ ]

(enter the same person from your daily shadow work)

SHADOW INTEGRATION:

Below, accept & reclaim the shadow chacterter traits that had the greatest emotional impact on you from your daily shadow work AND include what the purpose or role those traits play in your life now.

(defense mechanism/self preservation etc.)

Beacuse of you, I now realize that I AM:

DATE ____/____/____   **STEP** 1

Daily Shadow Work Prompt:

Who evoked the biggest emotional response from you today? Who triggered you?

[ ]

(family member/friend/stranger/movie character etc.)

Describe 5 of the person's character traits:

- -
- -
- -
- -
- -

Now go back and add the words "I AM" in front of each character trait above.

Which trait evoked the greatest resistance in you? Which did you feel defensive about? Allow the feelings to flow through you with self awareness of how you're feeling.

What is the oldest memory you have of when you felt that same way?
(the underlying trauma that the feelings stem from)

What would you say to your inner child if you could be there during the underyling trauma with the wisdom you have now. Show love & nurture your inner child.

STEP 3 – Cut along the dotted line, thank the person who triggered your shadow work, read out loud what you wrote in STEP 2 . Lastly release your negative resistence to your shadow by burning STEP 1

DATE _____/_____/_____ **STEP** 2

Daily Illumination Prompt:

Today, I am deeply grateful that this person has helped me to bring light to my shadow.

[ ]

(enter the same person from your daily shadow work)

DATE _____/_____/_____ **STEP** 1

Daily Shadow Work Prompt:

Who evoked the biggest emotional response from you today? Who triggered you?

[ ]

(family member/friend/stranger/movie character etc.)

SHADOW INTEGRATION:

Below, accept & reclaim the shadow chacterter traits that had the greatest emotional impact on you from your daily shadow work AND include what the purpose or role those traits play in your life now.

(defense mechanism/self preservation etc.)

Beacuse of you, I now realize that I AM:

Describe 5 of the person's character traits:

-
-
-
-
-

Now go back and add the words "I AM" in front of each character trait above.

Which trait evoked the greatest resistance in you? Which did you feel defensive about? Allow the feelings to flow through you with self awareness of how you're feeling.

What is the oldest memory you have of when you felt that same way?
(the underlying trauma that the feelings stem from)

What would you say to your inner child if you could be there during the underyling trauma with the wisdom you have now. Show love & nurture your inner child.

STEP 3 — Cut along the dotted line, thank the person who triggered your shadow work, read out loud what you wrote in STEP 2 . Lastly release your negative resistence to your shadow by burning STEP 1

Daily Illumination Prompt:

Today, I am deeply grateful that this person has helped me to bring light to my shadow.

(enter the same person from your daily shadow work)

Daily Shadow Work Prompt:

Who evoked the biggest emotional response from you today? Who triggered you?

(family member/friend/stranger/movie character etc.)

SHADOW INTEGRATION:

Below, accept & reclaim the shadow chacterter traits that had the greatest emotional impact on you from your daily shadow work AND include what the purpose or role those traits play in your life now.

(defense mechanism/self preservation etc.)

Beacuse of you, I now realize that I AM:

Describe 5 of the person's character traits:

-
-
-
-
-

Now go back and add the words "I AM" in front of each character trait above.

Which trait evoked the greatest resistence in you? Which did you feel defensive about? Allow the feelings to flow through you with self awareness of how you're feeling.

What is the oldest memory you have of when you felt that same way?
(the underlying trauma that the feelings stem from)

What would you say to your inner child if you could be there during the underyling trauma with the wisdom you have now. Show love & nurture your inner child.

STEP 3 — Cut along the dotted line, thank the person who triggered your shadow work, read out loud what you wrote in STEP 2 . Lastly release your negative resistence to your shadow by burning STEP 1

Daily Illumination Prompt:

Today, I am deeply grateful that this person has helped me to bring light to my shadow.

(enter the same person from your daily shadow work)

SHADOW INTEGRATION:

Below, accept & reclaim the shadow chacterter traits that had the greatest emotional impact on you from your daily shadow work AND include what the purpose or role those traits play in your life now.

(defense mechanism/self preservation etc.)

Beacuse of you, I now realize that I AM:

Daily Shadow Work Prompt:

Who evoked the biggest emotional response from you today? Who triggered you?

(family member/friend/stranger/movie character etc.)

Describe 5 of the person's character traits:

-
-
-
-
-

Now go back and add the words "I AM" in front of each character trait above.

Which trait evoked the greatest resistance in you? Which did you feel defensive about? Allow the feelings to flow through you with self awareness of how you're feeling.

What is the oldest memory you have of when you felt that same way?
(the underlying trauma that the feelings stem from)

What would you say to your inner child if you could be there during the underyling trauma with the wisdom you have now. Show love & nurture your inner child.

STEP 3 — Cut along the dotted line, thank the person who triggered your shadow work, read out loud what you wrote in STEP 2 . Lastly release your negative resistence to your shadow by burning STEP 1

DATE ____/___/____ **STEP** 2

Daily Illumination Prompt:

Today, I am deeply grateful that this person has helped me to bring light to my shadow.

[ ]

(enter the same person from your daily shadow work)

SHADOW INTEGRATION:

Below, accept & reclaim the shadow chacterter traits that had the greatest emotional impact on you from your daily shadow work AND include what the purpose or role those traits play in your life now.
(defense mechanism/self preservation etc.)

Beacuse of you, I now realize that I AM:

STEP 3 — Cut along the dotted line, thank the person who triggered your shadow work, read out loud what you wrote in STEP 2 . Lastly release your negative resistence to your shadow by burning STEP 1

DATE ____/___/____ **STEP** 1

Daily Shadow Work Prompt:

Who evoked the biggest emotional response from you today? Who triggered you?

[ ]

(family member/friend/stranger/movie character etc.)

Describe 5 of the person's character traits:

-
-
-
-
-

Now go back and add the words "I AM" in front of each character trait above.

Which trait evoked the greatest resistance in you? Which did you feel defensive about? Allow the feelings to flow through you with self awareness of how you're feeling.

What is the oldest memory you have of when you felt that same way?
(the underlying trauma that the feelings stem from)

What would you say to your inner child if you could be there during the underyling trauma with the wisdom you have now. Show love & nurture your inner child.

Daily Illumination Prompt:

Today, I am deeply grateful that this person has helped me to bring light to my shadow.

(enter the same person from your daily shadow work)

Daily Shadow Work Prompt:

Who evoked the biggest emotional response from you today? Who triggered you?

(family member/friend/stranger/movie character etc.)

SHADOW INTEGRATION:

Below, accept & reclaim the shadow chacterter traits that had the greatest emotional impact on you from your daily shadow work AND include what the purpose or role those traits play in your life now.

(defense mechanism/self preservation etc.)

Beacuse of you, I now realize that I AM:

Describe 5 of the person's character traits:

-
-
-
-
-

Now go back and add the words "I AM" in front of each character trait above.

Which trait evoked the greatest resistance in you? Which did you feel defensive about? Allow the feelings to flow through you with self awareness of how you're feeling.

What is the oldest memory you have of when you felt that same way?
(the underlying trauma that the feelings stem from)

What would you say to your inner child if you could be there during the underyling trauma with the wisdom you have now. Show love & nurture your inner child.

STEP 3

- Cut along the dotted line, thank the person who triggered your shadow work, read out loud what you wrote in STEP 2 . Lastly release your negative resistence to your shadow by burning STEP 1

Daily Illumination Prompt:

Today, I am deeply grateful that this person has helped me to bring light to my shadow.

[ ]

(enter the same person from your daily shadow work)

Daily Shadow Work Prompt:

Who evoked the biggest emotional response from you today? Who triggered you?

[ ]

(family member/friend/stranger/movie character etc.)

SHADOW INTEGRATION:

Below, accept & reclaim the shadow chacterter traits that had the greatest emotional impact on you from your daily shadow work AND include what the purpose or role those traits play in your life now.

(defense mechanism/self preservation etc.)

Beacuse of you, I now realize that I AM:

Describe 5 of the person's character traits:

- -
- -
- -
- -
- -

Now go back and add the words "I AM" in front of each character trait above.

Which trait evoked the greatest resistance in you? Which did you feel defensive about? Allow the feelings to flow through you with self awareness of how you're feeling.

What is the oldest memory you have of when you felt that same way?
(the underlying trauma that the feelings stem from)

What would you say to your inner child if you could be there during the underyling trauma with the wisdom you have now. Show love & nurture your inner child.

STEP 3 — Cut along the dotted line, thank the person who triggered your shadow work, read out loud what you wrote in STEP 2 . Lastly release your negative resistence to your shadow by burning STEP 1

DATE ____/____/____   **STEP** 2

Daily Illumination Prompt:

Today, I am deeply grateful that this person has helped me to bring light to my shadow.

```
┌─────────────────────────────────────┐
│                                     │
└─────────────────────────────────────┘
```

(enter the same person from your daily shadow work)

SHADOW INTEGRATION:

Below, accept & reclaim the shadow chacterter traits that had the greatest emotional impact on you from your daily shadow work AND include what the purpose or role those traits play in your life now.

(defense mechanism/self preservation etc.)

Beacuse of you, I now realize that I AM:

DATE ____/____/____   **STEP** 1

Daily Shadow Work Prompt:

Who evoked the biggest emotional response from you today? Who triggered you?

```
┌─────────────────────────────────────┐
│                                     │
└─────────────────────────────────────┘
```

(family member/friend/stranger/movie character etc.)

Describe 5 of the person's character traits:

-
-
-
-
-

Now go back and add the words "I AM" in front of each character trait above.

Which trait evoked the greatest resistance in you? Which did you feel defensive about? Allow the feelings to flow through you with self awareness of how you're feeling.

What is the oldest memory you have of when you felt that same way?
(the underlying trauma that the feelings stem from)

What would you say to your inner child if you could be there during the underyling trauma with the wisdom you have now. Show love & nurture your inner child.

STEP 3 – Cut along the dotted line, thank the person who triggered your shadow work, read out loud what you wrote in STEP 2 . Lastly release your negative resistence to your shadow by burning STEP 1

DATE ____/____/____ **STEP 2**

Daily Illumination Prompt:

Today, I am deeply grateful that this person has helped me to bring light to my shadow.

[ ]

(enter the same person from your daily shadow work)

SHADOW INTEGRATION:

Below, accept & reclaim the shadow chacterter traits that had the greatest emotional impact on you from your daily shadow work AND include what the purpose or role those traits play in your life now.

(defense mechanism/self preservation etc.)

Beacuse of you, I now realize that I AM:

DATE ____/____/____ **STEP 1**

Daily Shadow Work Prompt:

Who evoked the biggest emotional response from you today? Who triggered you?

[ ]

(family member/friend/stranger/movie character etc.)

Describe 5 of the person's character traits:

-
-
-
-
-

Now go back and add the words "I AM" in front of each character trait above.

Which trait evoked the greatest resistance in you? Which did you feel defensive about? Allow the feelings to flow through you with self awareness of how you're feeling.

What is the oldest memory you have of when you felt that same way?
(the underlying trauma that the feelings stem from)

What would you say to your inner child if you could be there during the underyling trauma with the wisdom you have now. Show love & nurture your inner child.

STEP 3 – Cut along the dotted line, thank the person who triggered your shadow work, read out loud what you wrote in STEP 2 . Lastly release your negative resistence to your shadow by burning STEP 1

DATE ____/____/____   STEP 2 | DATE ____/____/____   STEP 1

Daily Illumination Prompt:

Today, I am deeply grateful that this person has helped me to bring light to my shadow.

[   ]

(enter the same person from your daily shadow work)

Daily Shadow Work Prompt:

Who evoked the biggest emotional response from you today? Who triggered you?

[   ]

(family member/friend/stranger/movie character etc.)

SHADOW INTEGRATION:

Below, accept & reclaim the shadow chacterter traits that had the greatest emotional impact on you from your daily shadow work AND include what the purpose or role those traits play in your life now.

(defense mechanism/self preservation etc.)

Beacuse of you, I now realize that I AM:

Describe 5 of the person's character traits:

-
-
-
-
-

Now go back and add the words "I AM" in front of each character trait above.

Which trait evoked the greatest resistence in you? Which did you feel defensive about? Allow the feelings to flow through you with self awareness of how you're feeling.

What is the oldest memory you have of when you felt that same way?
(the underlying trauma that the feelings stem from)

What would you say to your inner child if you could be there during the underyling trauma with the wisdom you have now. Show love & nurture your inner child.

STEP 3 — Cut along the dotted line, thank the person who triggered your shadow work, read out loud what you wrote in STEP 2 . Lastly release your negative resistence to your shadow by burning STEP 1

DATE ____/____/____　　　　　　　　**STEP** 2 ┊ DATE ____/____/____　　　　　　　　**STEP** 1

Daily Illumination Prompt:

Today, I am deeply grateful that this person has helped me to bring light to my shadow.

```
┌─────────────────────────────────────┐
│                                     │
│                                     │
└─────────────────────────────────────┘
```

(enter the same person from your daily shadow work)

Daily Shadow Work Prompt:

Who evoked the biggest emotional response from you today? Who triggered you?

```
┌─────────────────────────────────────┐
│                                     │
│                                     │
└─────────────────────────────────────┘
```

(family member/friend/stranger/movie character etc.)

SHADOW INTEGRATION:

Below, accept & reclaim the shadow chacterter traits that had the greatest emotional impact on you from your daily shadow work AND include what the purpose or role those traits play in your life now.

(defense mechanism/self preservation etc.)

Beacuse of you, I now realize that I AM:

Describe 5 of the person's character traits:

-
-
-
-
-

Now go back and add the words "I AM" in front of each character trait above.

Which trait evoked the greatest resistance in you? Which did you feel defensive about? Allow the feelings to flow through you with self awareness of how you're feeling.

What is the oldest memory you have of when you felt that same way?
(the underlying trauma that the feelings stem from)

What would you say to your inner child if you could be there during the underyling trauma with the wisdom you have now. Show love & nurture your inner child.

STEP 3 — Cut along the dotted line, thank the person who triggered your shadow work, read out loud what you wrote in STEP 2 . Lastly release your negative resistence to your shadow by burning STEP 1

Printed in Great Britain
by Amazon